I CAN COOK

By Pam Cary
Illustrated by Kate Simpson

RD Publishing

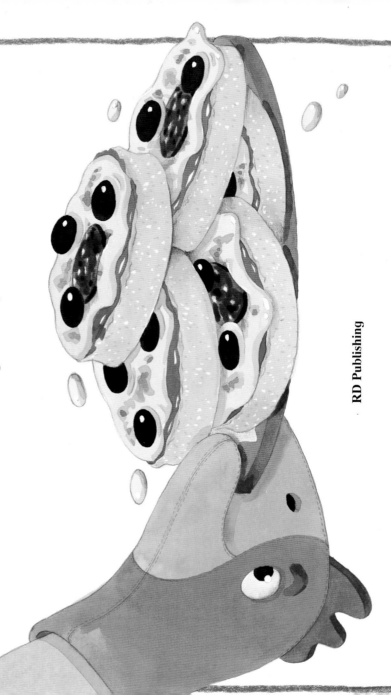

Cooking Words

Bake	■	Cook your food in an oven for as long as the recipe says.
Beat	■	Mix your ingredients together briskly with a spoon.
Boil	■	Heat a pot of water on the stove until the water bubbles.
Broil	■	Put the food under a hot broiler.
Chop	■	Cut the food into small pieces with a knife.
Cream	■	Stir the mixture briskly with a spoon until it is creamy.
Freeze	■	Put the food in a freezer until it has frozen solid.
Knead	■	Fold over and press the dough with your hands until it is smooth and stretchy.
Mash	■	Use the back of a fork or spoon to squash the food into a smooth paste.
Melt	■	Stir the ingredients in a pan on a warm stove until they become liquid.
Mix	■	Stir the ingredients together with a spoon.
Mold	■	Use your hands to shape the ingredients any way you want.
Sift	■	Put the ingredients through a sifter into a bowl.
Slice	■	Cut the food into even pieces.

With special thanks to: George, age 3; Jack, age 5; Nicola, age 5; Zoe, age 6; and Zara, age 7, for their help in testing the recipes.

RD Publishing Services
Reader's Digest Road, Pleasantville, NY 10570-7000
Copyright © 1995, 2000 Reader's Digest Children's Publishing Ltd
All rights reserved. Reader's Digest is a registered
trademark of The Reader's Digest Association, Inc.
Unauthorized reproduction, in any manner, is prohibited.
Manufactured in China
ISBN: 1-57584-668-3
2 4 6 8 10 9 7 5 3 1

Contents

Note to parents: Young children love to cook, but they do need supervision—particularly when using knives and hot stoves, broilers, and ovens. Allow for as much independence as possible, but remember that putting safety first helps to make cooking an exciting and positive learning experience.

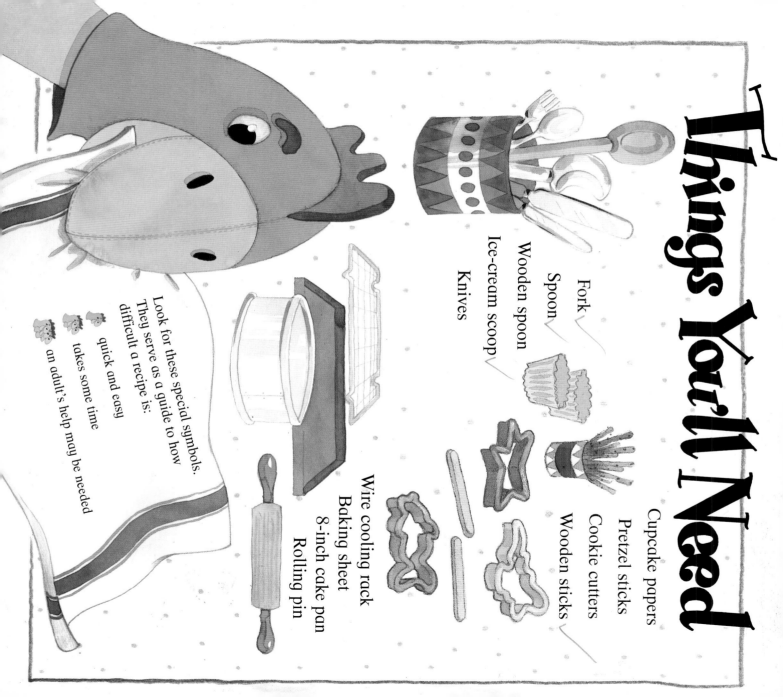

Things You'll Need

Fork
Spoon
Wooden spoon
Ice-cream scoop
Knives

Cupcake papers
Pretzel sticks
Cookie cutters
Wooden sticks

Wire cooling rack
Baking sheet
8-inch cake pan
Rolling pin

Look for these special symbols.
They serve as a guide to how
difficult a recipe is:

quick and easy

takes some time

an adult's help may be needed

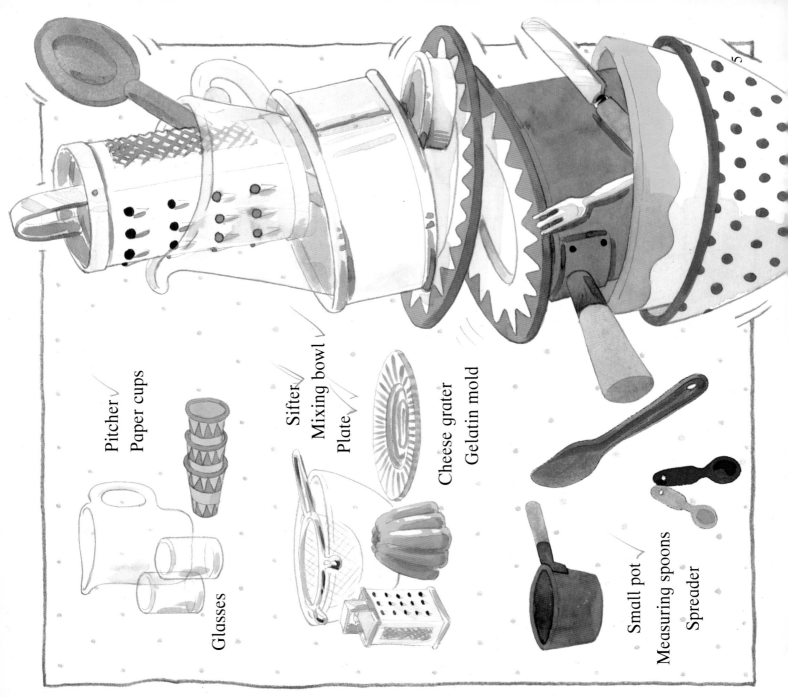

5

Pitcher ✓
Paper cups

Glasses

Sifter ✓
Mixing bowl ✓
Plate ✓

Cheese grater
Gelatin mold

Small pot ✓
Measuring spoons
Spreader

Sunshine Vegetable Dip

You will need:

- ½ cup (100 g) mayonnaise ▪ 6 teaspoons catsup ▪ 3 teaspoons chopped sweet or dill pickle (if you like) ▪ 4 carrots ▪ 1 cucumber
- 1 celery stalk

Step 1
Mix together the mayonnaise, the catsup, and the pickle in a bowl.

Step 2
Spoon the dip into a small bowl. Place the bowl in the middle of a large round plate.

Step 3
Wash the vegetables (and peel them, if you like). Cut the vegetables into 3-inch (8-cm) pieces, then cut the pieces into lengthwise strips. Arrange them around the bowl of dip.

Yummy Yoggie Ice-Pops

(makes about 16 cube ice-pops)

You will need: · ½ cup (150 ml) milk · ½ cup (150 g) unflavored yogurt
· 1 ripe banana · 2 teaspoons honey

Step 1
In a bowl, mix together the milk and the yogurt thoroughly with a wooden spoon. Peel the banana.

Step 2
Put the banana in a small bowl and mash it with a fork. Add the mashed banana and honey to the milk and beat the mixture.

Step 3
Pour the mixture into small cups or ice-cube trays. Put them stick into small paper Freeze the ice-pops. Push a Freeze the ice-pops in the freezer. hours until solid.

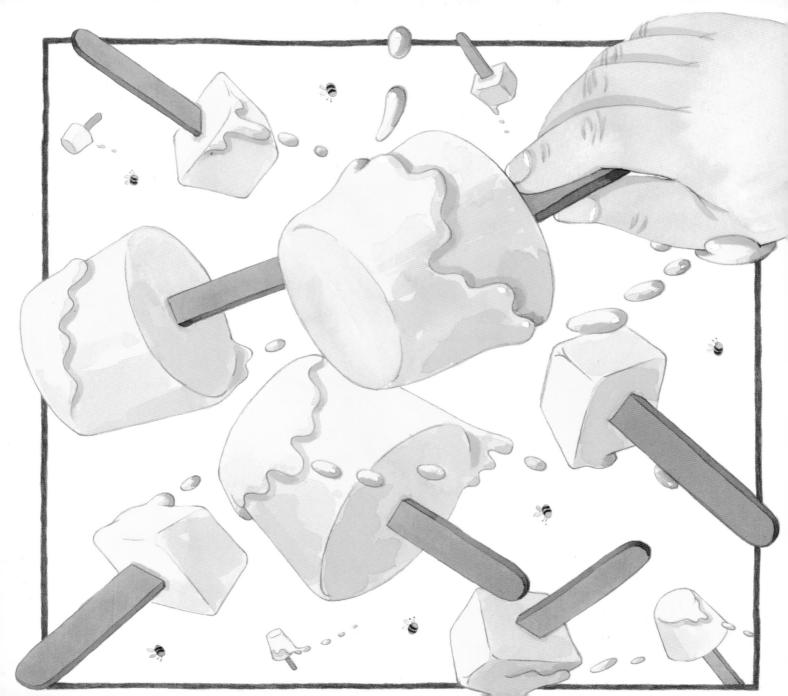

Sandwich Snails

(makes about 12 snails)

You will need:

- 4 large slices bread
- Peanut butter
- Strawberry or raspberry jelly
- 12 pretzel sticks
- 12 olives

Step 1
Cut the crusts off the bread. Use a rolling pin lightly to roll out the bread.

Step 2
Spread each slice of bread with a little peanut butter and jelly.

Use a dab of jelly on a strip of bread to hold your snail's shell upright. Add a pretzel stick and olive for its head.

Step 4
Cut each roll crosswise into 1-inch (2.5-cm) slices. Arrange the snails on a plate.

Step 3
Roll up each slice of bread tightly, like a jelly roll. Place the rolls on a flat surface with the "seams" underneath.

Whizzy Fizzy Drinks

For the Cranberry Float
you will need:

- 2 cups (455 ml) cranberry juice
- 2 cups (455 ml) seltzer
- Vanilla ice cream

For the Ginger and Apple Fizzy
you will need:

- 2 cups (455 ml) ginger ale
- 2 cups (455 ml) apple juice
- 1 apple
- Ice cubes

Step 1
To make Cranberry Float, use a long spoon to mix the cranberry juice and the seltzer in a pitcher.

Step 2
Pour the juice into 4 glasses. Scoop some ice cream into each glass.

Step 1
To make Ginger and Apple Fizzy, use a long spoon to mix the ginger ale and apple juice in a pitcher.

Step 2
Thinly slice the apple (you don't have to peel it) and add it to the pitcher. Add the ice cubes and pour the juice into 4 glasses.

Cream Cheese Boats

(makes 4 boats)

You will need:
- **2 slices ham**
- **½ cup (125 g) cream cheese, softened**
- **2 celery stalks**
- **2 slices of American cheese**
- **2 carrots**
- **Pretzel sticks**

Step 1
Chop the ham into little pieces. In a bowl, mix together the cream cheese and the ham.

Step 2
Wash the celery and cut it into 4-inch (10-cm) pieces. Fill the center of the celery pieces with the cream cheese mixture.

Step 3
Cut the American cheese into triangles. Wash or peel the carrots. Cut them into 1-inch (2.5-cm) pieces.

Step 4
To make tugboats, stick two carrot pieces into the cream cheese for the chimneys. To make sailboats, use pretzel sticks and cheese triangles to make sails.

Peppermint Mice

(makes about 12 mice)

You will need:
- 4 cups (500 g) confectioners' sugar
- 1 egg white
- 6 teaspoons water
- A few drops of red food coloring
- ½ teaspoon peppermint extract
- Almond halves
- Silver cake-decorating balls
- Licorice shoelaces

Step 1
In a bowl, knead together the sugar, the egg white, and the water. Add a few drops of food coloring and the peppermint extract. Mix together. Refrigerate 1 hour or until firm. Divide the mixture into 12 parts.

Step 2
Working quickly, mold each part of the mixture into a mouse body and peppermint head.

Step 3
Use the almond halves for ears, the silver balls for eyes and nose, and a piece of licorice for the tail. Mark whiskers with a pretzel stick.

Try using lemon or orange flavoring for different-tasting mice!

Eggy Crab

You will need:
- 1 egg • 3 teaspoons mayonnaise
- 1 pita bread • 2 carrots

Step 1
Ask an adult to carefully place the egg into a pot of boiling water and hard-boil the egg for 10 minutes.

Step 2
Use a spoon to remove the egg from the pot. Place the egg in a bowl of cold water. When cool, peel the egg.

Step 3
In a bowl, mash the egg with a fork. Mix in the mayonnaise. Slice the pita bread through the top only.

Step 4
Fill the pita bread with the egg mixture. Cut the carrots into strips. Place them around the pita to look like crab claws.

Fruit Mold

You will need:
- 1 package (3 ounces or 75 g) gelatin dessert
- 1 banana
- 1 cup fresh or canned sliced fruit

Step 1
Prepare the gelatin in a bowl or large measuring cup according to the instructions on the package.

Step 2
Peel and slice the banana. Gently stir the fruit into the gelatin.

Step 3
Pour the gelatin into a 2-cup (455-ml) mold. Place it in the refrigerator for 3–4 hours.

Step 4
To unmold the gelatin, quickly dip the mold into hot water, and turn over as a unit. Remove mold. place a plate on top of the mold.

If you don't have a gelatin mold, use a cup or yogurt carton.

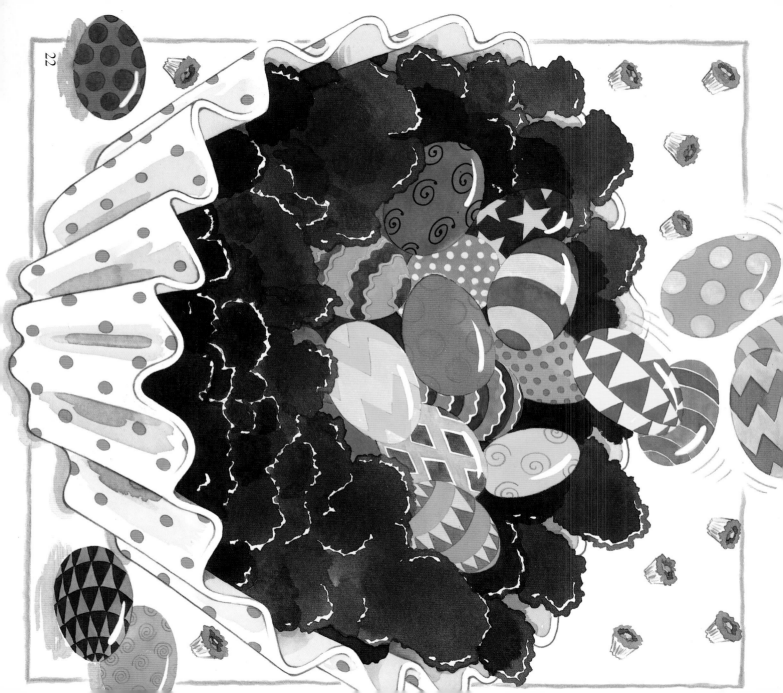

Chocolate Bird Nests

(makes about 12 nests)
You will need:

- 6 teaspoons (25 g) honey
- 6 teaspoons (25 g) butter
- 4 ounces (100 g) semisweet chocolate
- 3 cups (100 g) cornflakes
- Small chocolate candy eggs or other candies

Step 1
Place the honey, butter, and chocolate in a small pot over low heat. Stir with a spoon until the chocolate has melted. Remove from heat.

Step 2
Add the cornflakes and stir the mixture until the flakes are well-coated with chocolate.

Step 3
Press the cooled chocolate flakes against the sides of the cupcake papers, making a hole in the center. Let the nests stand 2 hours to set. Place colorful candies in each nest to look like birds' eggs.

Muffin Pizzas

(makes 4 pizzas)

You will need:

- 2 English muffins ■ A little butter or margarine
- ½ cup (75 g) tomato sauce ■ 1 cup (100 g) grated cheese

Step 1

Split each muffin into halves. Spread the inside of each half with a little butter or margarine. Place on a broiler tray.

Step 2

Ask an adult to place the muffins under a hot broiler until they are just brown.

Step 3

Spread each toasted muffin with a little tomato sauce. Sprinkle the cheese evenly over the top. Have an adult place the pizzas under the broiler until the cheese bubbles. Be very careful when removing the broiler until the cheese bubbles. Be very careful when removing the pizzas—they will be very hot!

If you like, in Step 3, add slices of pepperoni or olives before broiling.

Frosted Cake

You will need:
- ½ cup (100 g) butter or margarine, softened
- ½ cup (100 g) sugar ▪ 2 eggs
- 1 cup (125 g) all-purpose flour

For the frosting: ▪ 1¼ cups (155 g) confectioners' sugar
▪ 3–6 teaspoons warm water ▪ A few drops of food coloring

Step 1
Heat the oven to 400°F (200°C). In a bowl, cream together the butter and the sugar with a wooden spoon. Break the eggs into a small bowl and beat them with a fork.

Step 2
Mix the eggs into the mixture a little at a time. Sift in flour. Pour into a greased 8-inch (20-cm) cake pan. Bake for 15 to 20 minutes.

Step 3
Meanwhile, make the frosting. In a bowl, mix together the confectioners' sugar and the water. Mix in a few drops of food coloring.

Step 4
After baking, let the cake cool, then remove it from cake pan. Dip the spreader in warm water and spread the frosting over the top.

Cheese Shapes

You will need:

(makes 10–12 shapes)

- 1 ready-made uncooked pie shell • ½ cup (75 g) grated cheese • A little flour

Step 1

Heat the oven to 350°F (180°C). Place the uncooked pie shell in a bowl and knead it together with the cheese.

Step 2
Sprinkle a little flour over a flat surface. Place the dough mixture on the surface and gently roll it flat with a rolling pin.

Step 3
Using cookie cutters, cut out shapes from the dough. Re-roll any extra bits of dough to make more shapes.

Step 4
Put the dough shapes on a greased baking sheet and bake the shapes with a minutes. Remove the shapes with a spatula to a cooling rack.

Sugar-Chip Cookies

(makes 48–60 cookie...

You will need:

- 1 cup (225 g) butter or margarine, softened · 1 cup (220 g) sugar
- 1 egg · 2 cups (300 g) all-purpose flour · ½ teaspoon salt
- ½ teaspoon baking soda · ½ teaspoon cream of tartar
- 1 teaspoon vanilla · 2 cups (340 g) semisweet chocolate chips

Step 1
Heat the oven to 400°F (200°C). In a large bowl, beat the butter, sugar and egg together with a wooden spoon.

Step 2
Sift the flour, the salt, the baking soda, and the cream of tartar into the bowl; mix thoroughly. Mix in the vanilla and the chocolate chips.

Step 3
Drop spoonfuls of the cookie mixture about 3 inches (8 cm) apart onto a baking sheet. Flatten each cookie with a fork.

Step 4
Bake the cookies on the center rack for 8 to 10 minutes. Use a spatula to remove the cookies to a wire rack to cool.

Party Hints

Now that you are a cook, why not have a party? Invite your friends and family over to try your new recipes. Fill in the invitation cards and decorate them with fun, colorful stickers before you send them out.

Copy your favorite recipes on the recipe cards and keep them handy while you cook. Put stickers on the ones you like the most!

To make your party special, fill out the menu cards and place cards. Write down all the things you will be serving on the menu cards and put them on the table. Then write each person's name on a place card and put them near each person's plate.

And just in case things get messy, make sure to have napkins ready. Don't forget to use the beautiful napkin rings!

Now you are all set! Bon appétit!